The Empty Chair

A Thanksgiving Play For Youth

Raymond I. Keffer

CSS Publishing Company, Inc., Lima, Ohio

THE EMPTY CHAIR

For more information about CSS Publishing Company resources, visit our website at www.csspub.com.

ISBN: 978-0-7880-1833-6   PRINTED IN U.S.A.

The Empty Chair *is dedicated
to my loving wife Gail K. Keffer
and to the Reverend Doug Dorsey*

*and in memory of
Jean B. Keffer, mother
Jenny F. Kennedy, mother-in-law
Gertrude Forsythe, aunt
Miss Griffith, algebra teacher*

The Empty Chair

Cast

The cast is comprised of a pastor and four students who are on a local mission project packing Thanksgiving baskets for the poor of the community

Pastor Walsh: a youth pastor who leads by example in church functions or by working with the youth on special projects like this mission outreach

1st Person: a person in tenth or eleventh grade who was influenced as a ninth grader by a Bible-reading algebra teacher who in her vintage years led by example with her Christian love

2nd Person: a person in the seventh or eighth grade who loves history and has been influenced by the writings of our founding fathers, who pledged their lives, fortunes, and sacred honor as each signed the Declaration of Independence

3rd Person: a person in eighth or ninth grade who has had a wonderful relationship with grandparents, especially a grandmother who was a Christian witness throughout her life to her grandchild

4th Person: a person in eleventh or twelfth grade who is approaching adulthood with a perspective of how important family relationships are as he/she prepares to step out of the family circle for a life in college or at work

The young persons in the cast may be either male or female. The director is free to cast the person of either gender who is right for each part based on the character makeup of the individual.

Scene
   A local restaurant

Stage Setting

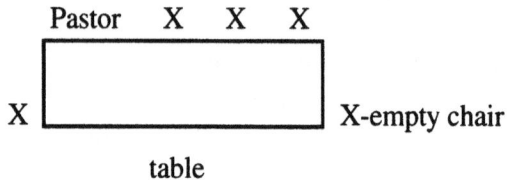

Pastor   X   X   X

X [table   ]   X-empty chair

Stage Level _____

   The pastor and young people are seated by a host and given menus. The youth sit in chairs (X) with the empty chair at the end of the table, which is set for six.

(The cast follows a hostess to their table, and each takes a seat around the table with an empty chair at the end of the table. The group looks at the menu left by the hostess)

1st Person: Wow! This is a neat restaurant, Pastor Walsh. I'm not sure that I have enough money to buy even a hamburger in this place.

Pastor: Relax, everyone, this meal is on me!

(Group shows approval)

Pastor: I'm very proud of how hard you all have worked in getting those food baskets ready for the poor these past two days. Tonight, I want you to have a good meal and a good night's rest before we begin delivering those baskets to the poor tomorrow.

2nd Person: Gee! Thank you, Pastor Walsh, you're very kind and understanding. *(Pauses, gives inquisitive look)* However, I have a question for you. You asked the hostess for a table for six ... and there are only five of us. How come?

(Group reacts, "Yes, why six?")

Pastor: It's true there are only five of us, but there might be a sixth person who may show up. You never know.

3rd Person: What do you mean, Pastor Walsh ... you never know?

Pastor: When eating out, you never know if you'll see a friend eating alone who can join you, or a stranger whom you met in line who is dining alone while waiting for your table to be prepared.

Haven't you ever been away from home, feeling down, and then by chance you run into someone you know or meet a person whom you feel that you have always known?

(Group reacts positively)

Pastor: The empty chair at this table is for a friend or that special person whom you may meet by chance. No one likes to eat alone. So the extra chair at this table is for those people.

On holidays or Sundays, my parents always set an extra place or two for guests. More often than not, an unexpected guest would come. When the table already has a place setting for an extra person, that person feels more welcome to join you. He doesn't feel he is interrupting your meal.

Do any of your parents set an extra place at your dinner table once in a while?

(Group looks at each other)

4th person: It's funny that you mention that, Pastor. Four or five times a year, my father asks my mother to set an extra place setting at the dining room table.

2nd Person: Really! What are those occasions when the extra place is set?

4th Person: Well, it may sound strange, *(Pauses)* but every Veterans' Day in November, Memorial Day in May, plus Easter, Thanksgiving, and Christmas.

1st Person: Veterans' Day? Memorial Day? Those are strange holidays for people to have an extra place setting at their table!

4th Person: It's not so strange when you understand that my Uncle Bob is an MIA from the Vietnam War!

1st Person: MIA! Oh, I'm sorry, I didn't know that your uncle was one of those who are still Missing In Action from that war. *(Pauses, head down. Looks up)* That must be a terrible burden for your family.

4th Person: Thank you. It's more of a burden for my father than for anyone else. My Uncle Bob was shot down over North Vietnam in November, 1972. His buddies saw him eject from his plane, and parachute safely to the ground into a rice paddy. That's the last time he was seen alive. He was never heard from again. You see, it was common for Vietnamese farmers to murder pilots in their fields if soldiers did not get to the American pilot first.

My uncle was an Annapolis graduate who lived the military. My father was exempt from the draft then, as he was a college student who married while in college, so he never served in the military.

My dad and my uncle felt they had different calls in life when it came to the military. They respected each other's decision about it. My father told me that his brother never feared death. He often told my dad, as a Marine pilot and as an American, that he would be willing to give up his life to keep his family and our nation free.

Pastor: I understand what your uncle was saying. John 15:13 says it all: "Greater love hath no man than to lay down his life for his friends." Your Uncle Bob was willing to die so that his family and nation would remain free. What a beautiful tribute to his family and nation. (*Pauses*)

So the empty chair on those holidays is to honor the life of your uncle who remains an MIA? Right?

4th Person: Right. When I have my own home, I will continue this tradition to honor my Uncle Bob. My father still hopes that some day my uncle will return from Vietnam. He has never given up hope that some day my Uncle Bob will knock on our front door again.

1st Person: That's a beautiful story. We need to pray for your uncle and all the MIAs even though that has long ago ended for us. (*Pauses*)

I have a favorite scriptural song from the Vietnam era. Maybe you have heard this song and the lyrics before:

> *For every season,*
> *Turn, turn, turn,*

9

There is a reason,
Turn, turn, turn.
A time to live,
A time to die,
A time to laugh
A time to cry.
A time for everything, under heaven.

Pastor: Wait, I know those lyrics, they're taken from Ecclesiastes 3: "To everything there is a season, and a time to every purpose under heaven. A time to be born, and a time to die; a time to plant and a time to pluck up that which is planted. A time to kill, and a time to heal ... a time to mourn, and a time to dance. A time to cast away stones, and a time to gather stones together, and a time to embrace and a time to refrain from embracing ... A time to keep silent and a time to speak. A time to love and a time to hate; a time of war, a time of peace." (*Pauses*)

How is it you know that song and scripture?

1st Person: I learned those words from my algebra teacher in school. On the first day in her class, she read to us from Ecclesiastes.

2nd Person: You can't be serious. Teachers are not allowed to read from the Bible in school any more thanks to the activist atheists.

1st Person: You and I know that, but she was an older teacher who felt that her students needed these words despite what the court system said. Her first lesson for us was not math, but a lesson in life. She said that since we were in high school now, we naturally thought we were something. (*Pauses*)

She said we were all special people at a special time in our lives. She said that we should enjoy the age we were and not to try to dress and act older. Age will come soon enough, she said, and that we should be happy for each stage of school life as it comes to us naturally. Let the seniors be seniors; enjoy being a freshman and the new challenges and opportunities which being a freshman can provide us.

Pastor: Did you believe what she had to say to you about life?

1st Person: At first, no! I thought she was a kook. But during the school year, I found out what a caring, forthright person she was. I started to pay heed to what she had said. I had a great freshman year thanks to her. For everything there was a season, just as she said. I grew up a lot that year.

I'd be most happy to save the place for her at my table so she could join us at any season of the year.

4th Person: Well, call her when you get home, and invite her over for Thanksgiving dinner.

1st Person: I'd like to do that, (*Pauses*) but the season came for her to be called home. (*Pauses*) She was a great lady. I will always have a seat at my table for her because of the goals for life she shared with me.

3rd Person: She must have been a wonderful lady to have had such an influence on your life that you can recall those verses from Ecclesiastes. Your teacher would have gotten along with my grandmother. (*Pauses*) Now, there was a saint!

2nd Person: Go on! Do you know what a saint is?

3rd Person: Yes! A saint is my grandmother. She was always doing things for others instead of herself. She always put the needs of others ahead of her own needs.

People would take advantage of her all the time, but she kept on helping them and turning the other cheek when they let her down. Some called her a doormat over which people walked. In times of need, she was the first there to help in a genuine, loving way.

At church, she was the one who always had an extra setting at her table for the visiting minister, missionary, or anyone else who was alone. I can still hear my mother talk about her, "Well, they asked at church today if anyone would like to have the guest missionary for dinner." My grandmother would always volunteer first. She always had room at her table for guests and a soft spot in her heart for others.

1st Person: Is that really true?

3rd Person: Indeed, it is true. No matter how many strangers or family members dropped by, there was always plenty of food and fellowship at Grandma's house to invite them to stay. Why, she could have fed the 5,000 all by herself and still have had cherry pie for dessert for all of them.

Pastor: I'm sure that she could. I think I read about her in Matthew 5:8: "Blessed are the pure in heart, for they shall see God." People perceived your grandmother's love and generosity as a weakness, when it was really a gift from God.

3rd Person: Indeed, it was a gift from God that she possessed, Pastor. She was a saint in every sense of the word.

4th Person: Wow! Those are some great people to save an extra place for at your table: a grandmother, an uncle, and a teacher.
  I don't have memories such as those. I guess that I must have missed something in my life.

Pastor: Not necessarily. If you had not given thought to saving a place at your table for a special guest, that doesn't mean that you have missed something. I'm sure that if any one of us were to drop by your home at meal time, we would be welcome to stay for a meal.

4th Person: Of course you would all be welcome at any time at our home to stay for a meal.

Pastor: You see, we all have different thoughts and ideas about people who have left impressions on us. In your case, I'm sure that many people have left definite impressions on you, but you have not had reason to focus in on any one person who has impressed you as these three people have influenced the others.

4th Person: In this case, Pastor, I think you're right. But thinking about this idea, I've always appreciated what the founding fathers of our nation did for us. It was they who made it possible for us to be able to celebrate both Thanksgiving and our freedom.

Pastor: Is there any one of the founding fathers who, more than the others, has impressed you?

4th Person: There are several: William Bradford, the governor of the Plymouth colony; Ann Hutchinson, the first woman evangelist; Ben Franklin, the first American. But, I've always admired John Adams the most.

In 1775 he was about the only voice that constantly called for independence at the Continental Congress. He was said to be obnoxious, stubborn, and pig-headed, but his wife Abigail said he was neither stubborn or obnoxious. (*Pauses*)

He helped to write the Declaration of Independence, and he and the others who signed that marvelous document, pledged their lives, their fortunes, and sacred trust at the same time. He had total commitment to God and to America.

2nd Person: Hmmm, (*Thinks*) lives, fortunes, sacred trust. That's some commitment, all right.

4th Person: His wife Abigail also said of him, "There's my husband John, who is always the first in line to be hanged."

John Adams was our first Vice President and second President of the United States. He was one of those sacrificing, wise persons who founded our nation. Such patriots would have a place of honor at my table, much like the special place you have for your Uncle Bob.

Pastor: Wisdom, yes, Colossians 4:5-6 says, "Walk in wisdom toward them that are without ... Let your speech be always with grace, seasoned with salt, that you may know how you ought to answer every man." John Adams may have had too much seasoning in his speech for some folk, but no one could doubt the wisdom in his commitment and love of God and America.

You have all made interesting choices as to whom the extra place setting at your table would go. Is it an accident that none of you chose Christ himself as your extra guest?

3rd Person: Oh, I never thought of Jesus! I thought of my grandmother first. I miss her. You know she still made the best cherry pie.

2nd Person: I should have thought of Jesus. After all, he is the perfect example as to how we should lead our lives. I just wasn't thinking. I just naturally thought of a person who influenced my life at a time when I was growing into adulthood.

1st Person: You're right, Pastor. Our family has been so involved with the MIAs and my uncle, my thoughts went automatically to him. Jesus would be welcome in our home as well as everyone's home who is sitting at this table now!

4th Person: Well, I had the biggest goof. I admired a man I never met, only in books. I knew he was a man of Christian principles, but I should have thought of the one person who set those principles, Jesus himself.

Pastor: You are all looking at your guest choice in the wrong light now. All of these people reflected some or many of the attributes which Christ himself had while he lived on earth. When you invite God's people to have dinner with you, you invited God also. All of your choices were God's people. Remember, Jesus said if you have done kind things for *my people*, you have done them for *me*.

You shall have dinner with your uncle, your grandmother, your algebra teacher, and John Adams when you too are redeemed. All those who mentioned are now with Jesus in their heavenly mansions. In John 14:2 Jesus said, "In my father's house are many mansions, if it were not so, I would have told you. I go to prepare a place for you." So as we prepare a place for Jesus or his people at our table, we are doing on earth what Jesus did here and what he is doing for us in Heaven. So let us rejoice at our meal this evening by praising God and giving thanks. Let's hold hands around the table and recite the Doxology together.

All: Praise God from whom all blessings flow.
Praise him all creatures here below.
Praise him above ye heavenly hosts.
Praise Father, Son, and Holy Ghost.

Pastor: Father, come be our guest at this table in the empty chair, and bless this food and fellowship which you have provided for us. Amen!

www.ingramcontent.com/pod-product-compliance
Lightning Source LLC
Chambersburg PA
CBHW070044040426
42331CB00033B/2503